FEED YOUR MIND

A STORY OF AUGUST WILSON

BY **JEN BRYANT** ILLUSTRATED BY **CANNADAY CHAPMAN**

ACT ONE
THE HILL DISTRICT, PITTSBURGH

They call it "Little Harlem"—the city within a city.
A mile east of downtown, it is a mishmash,
a melting pot of workers and their kin—
    Syrians, Africans, Poles, and Jews,
        Irish, Haitians, Germans, and Italians—
            their row homes, apartments, and shacks
                jam-packed between sloping streets.

On April 27, 1945, in a tiny apartment behind Bella's Market,
Frederick August Kittel Jr. is born. Named for his father,
a white German baker, who sometimes visits
with bread in his hand
but mostly is not around.

Now, Freddy walks down Wylie Avenue
with his mother, Daisy Wilson,
past barbers, butcher shops, bakeries,
where people speak Italian, Hebrew, or Greek,
their unique voices blending like an orchestra,
their smells (corned beef, lamb, okra, fettuccini!)
making his small mouth water.
Summer nights in the backyard, Daisy plays
card games with the neighbors as someone
strums a guitar, their laughter drifting over children
playing dodgeball and stickball—loading the bases.

Freddy plays, but he's an observer, too:
always watching and listening.
When night falls and the children are called inside,
he notices how most of them have
a mother *and* a father to tuck them in.
But not Freddy. Instead, with just a sixth-grade education
and a job cleaning other people's homes,
Daisy reads to him at night, filling him up
with stories, words, and hope: *"If you can read,*
you can do anything—you can **be** *anything."*

BREAKING THE CODE

Loops and lines in long, neat rows—
but what do they *mean*?
Mother reads . . . *she* knows.
He likes to turn the pages, feel the lightness of paper.
"Look here, Freddy," she says, pointing
to labels. His eyes follow her finger to the shelf,
his mouth sounding them out:
soup, tomato, rice, beans.
He is smart, curious. He is four.
One morning on the way out the door,
he spies Sister's schoolbook, open on the floor:

"The sun's light brings the leaves out."
—and suddenly the loops and lines begin to *mean*.
Each day after, he practices—textbooks,
newspapers, street signs, clothing labels—
drinking the words in faster and faster.
By the time he turns five, he even reads breakfast:
"Golden Yellow and ready to spread—Parkay!"
"Strawberry Jam. Smucker Company, the brand you can trust."
"Post's Grape-Nuts Flakes . . . it's Hopalong Cassidy's favorite whole-wheat cereal!"
Mother stops her washing. She looks at the table,
then back at her word-loving son.
"Get your coat, Freddy. We're going out."

WYLIE AVENUE BRANCH,
CARNEGIE LIBRARY OF PITTSBURGH

Tall walls. Big windows.
People sitting at long tables, whispering.
Rows and rows and rows of shelves!
"One moment, please," says the blue sweater
behind the counter.
Mother squeezes his hand. "I'll wait. You go on and pick out a book."
Running over to the shelf, his fingers glide
along the cool spines. He slides one out, brings it
to Mother, who shows him
a small card printed with his name.
"This means you can borrow any book in this room.
Is that the one you want?" It is.
Later . . .
his eyes move across the page,
following each line into a bright new world.

"WHEN IT RAINS, IT POURS"

"Morton Salt!" Mother cries out her answer
to the radio game: *Name the product that uses this slogan . . .*
and you win a brand-new washing machine!
A dime hurried into his sister's hand,
Sister running down to the pay phone on the corner,
calling the number, shouting into the receiver: "Morton Salt!"
A voice on the other end:
"Please stay on the line so we can get your name."
Jumping joy and jubilation!!! No more scrubboard
for Mother. No more bleeding, peeling hands.
His sister tries to stay calm, saying the family name
and address. "Where, miss? Say it again?"
She repeats . . . and *click*—swift as an electric switch—
that new machine vanishes.
Instead, the man says, *You get a certificate to the Salvation Army.*
They have some used ones there.
The slow, shuffle-walk home, his sister thinks on how
to soften the news: *But Mother, isn't that better than nothing?*
Better than having your back and wrists sore, your hands bleeding?
At least you won't be scrubbing no more . . .
Mother stirs soup, her silent rage rising with the steam.
"Tell them I said no. They can *keep* their used machine!"

RELOCATION

For twelve years, Freddy has known only
these two rooms (and an outhouse in back)
as *home*. Now, the city's building a new
civic center right smack in the Lower Hill,
so the Kittels move . . . to Hazelwood.
Bigger place, nicer place. Indoor plumbing.
Polish, Irish, Slovak, Hungarian, Italian—
most of the neighbors work in the steel mill.
Most are kind, welcoming.
Most—but not all.

C–R–A–S–H!! comes the brick through the window—
the note attached says "Nigger Stay Out."
Is Daisy afraid? . . . Ha! It'll take a lot more
than a brick and some scribbling to make her shake!
Next day, the newspaper prints the story
of the brick flying through their window.
Daisy reads that paper, then wraps it around
the note and the brick and throws it
out back in the trash.

DETOUR

At fourteen, he reads everything—
the family bible (minus the "begats"),
his sister's Hardy Boys books,
his other sister's Nancy Drews—
magazines, newspapers, sometimes even
an owner's manual or two. He reads
history books with battle maps and the letters
of Emperor Napoleon. He reads about
athletes: the boxer Floyd Patterson
and Pittsburgh's Negro League baseball teams,
the Crawfords and the Grays, whose players grew up
playing stickball on the Hill District streets.
One day, on the way home from the park,
he detours, bouncing his basketball to the door
of the Hazelwood Library. Inside, he finds
thirty or forty titles lined up on a shelf
labeled "Negro Books."
He mouths the names on the spines:
Hughes, Dunbar, Ellison, Wright.
The basketball becomes a chair,
the Dunbar book open on his lap:

"Be proud, my Race, in mind and soul;
Thy name is writ on Glory's scroll
In characters of fire."

The words make his heart skip.
Freddy reads right through supper, as all
around him the world shifts,
the universe opens wide.

SCHOOLED

Good grades get Freddy in.
He is the only
black student in ninth grade
at Central Catholic High.

Brother Dominic teaches English.
"This is good," Brother D tells Freddy,
handing back his homework.
"You could be a writer."

Meanwhile, each morning,
there's an unsigned note
on Freddy's desk:
"Go Home Nigger."

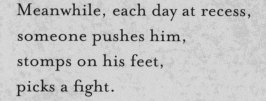

Meanwhile, each day at recess,
someone pushes him,
stomps on his feet,
picks a fight.

Freddy Kittel is big—
one hundred seventy-five pounds
of frustration and anger—but still
just one against the rest.

Most afternoons he finds
forty white kids waiting outside,
daring him
to try to walk by.

Sometimes, it's so
bad that the principal
puts Freddy in a cab,
sends him home.

Freddy thinks: *It's only
ninth grade. Three more years—
who can live
like this??*

"I quit," he tells the principal.
"Please don't," the principal says.
"I quit," he tells Brother Dominic.
"Please stay," says Brother D.

But when the principal goes back to his office and Brother D goes back to his class, Freddy just walks out.

NOW WHAT?

Her mouth is set hard, hands
    pounding on flour and lard.
"You are smart, Freddy . . .
    Now what?"

He shrugs, tries to read a book. She
    pounds harder on the dough.
"Well, if you're not gonna be a lawyer,
    then go

and learn how to fix cars or
    something." But at
Connelley trade school,
    all the auto classes are full.

Well, sheet metal then: tin cups and
    all kinds of metal stuff,
mechanical drawing class plus English,
    history and math.

But, wait a minute . . . these are
    fourth-grade books!!
Some kids *are fifteen and can't read.*
    This is my education?

"This isn't workin' out," he tells
    Mother. She shakes her head,
points across the street to Gladstone
    Public High: "Last chance."

So he goes, sits in the back—
    indifferent, frustrated. *More*
of the same, he thinks. Black
    and white kids may share

the room, but the blacks are still
    second-class.
The name-calling, the fights,
    the stares—the same here

as everywhere. He daydreams of
    Sonny Liston, the black
boxer who knocks out every white guy
    he fights.

Then—a miracle in history class!
    Write a paper on someone
from the past you admire. Freddy's eager
    to show what he knows.

For a week, he spends after-school
    hours at the library—reading,
taking notes, and writing
    "Napoleon's Will to Power."

He binds the pages, hands it in,
    feeling like maybe,
just maybe, this new school might be
    OK after all.

PROVE IT!

Teacher: You wrote this paper on Napoleon?

Freddy: Yes.

Teacher: The whole thing?

Freddy: Yes.

Teacher (*flipping through pages*): All twenty pages—all by yourself?

Freddy: Yes.

Teacher: You didn't copy it straight from a book?

Freddy: No. . . . I told you, I wrote it.

Teacher (*flipping through more pages, then pointing*): This part right here, where it talks about the battle . . . your older sister didn't write that?

Freddy (*looking at the passage*): No. I wrote it all myself. Those are *my* thoughts.

Teacher (*points to letter A and letter E at the top of the first page*):
I'm going to give you one of these two grades. You need to *prove* to me somehow that you wrote this paper.

Freddy (*frustrated*): I *told* you I wrote it. My footnotes and my sources are right there. Right *there*! I don't have to do more than that.

Teacher is silent. Thinking. Picks up pen and circles E, for failure, on the paper. Hands it to Freddy.

Freddy is disgusted. Angry. Trembling. Rips up paper and jams it in the wastebasket. Storms out of the room and out of the school.

I TOLD you I wrote it! I TOLD you
I TOLD you I wrote it! I TOLD you
I TOLD you I wrote it! I TOLD you I
I TOLD you I wrote it! I TOLD you I
I TOLD you I wrote it! I TOLD you I
I TOLD you I TOLD you I
I TOLD I TOLD you
I TOLD you I TOLD you I
I TOLD you I TOLD you I
I TOLD you

ACT TWO
ROWS

Like every other morning, he wakes, dresses, eats.
(He doesn't mention he's quit school *again*.)
Like every other morning, he leaves the house, walks
to the corner and across the street.
But this morning, his feet keep going north, toward Oakland.
"I dropped out of school, but I didn't
drop out of life." Many blocks later, he arrives at the
main branch of the Carnegie Public Library.
"If you can read, you can do anything." That's what Mother,
who had to quit school to work the crop rows
with *her* mother, said. Now, walking through *these* rows, Freddy
feels the weight of that story. He turns the corner
. . . and *there!* Hughes, Dunbar, Ellison, Wright—books by black
writers he'd found by chance back at the Hazelwood Branch.
And there are more: *W. E. B. Du Bois, Arna Bontemps, James Baldwin,*
Booker T. Washington—a mother lode of black literature,
a treasure he's aching to explore. Inside Ellison's *Invisible Man* he reads:
". . . I always tried to go in everyone's way but my own. I have
also been called one thing and then another while no one really wished
to hear what I called myself." *Yes,* yes!! Freddy whispers back to the book.
He reads the words again, slips off his shoes, lets that last line
lodge deep in his mind, a tool he will someday
pull out again—and use.

FEED YOUR MIND

Weekdays, he stays in Oakland till the schoolkids
go home. Mother doesn't know where he goes
(or if she does, she doesn't say).
All morning and half the afternoon, he reads those books

by black writers, but he also reads
about photography, history, art,
cooking, baseball, and antique cars;
he reads about religion, science, and philosophy.

He reads pages of the dictionary
and the World Book encyclopaedia,
the United States Constitution,
and the Emancipation Proclamation.

He reads with delight and with a fearsome hunger,
like a guest at a royal feast,
the table so wide, so vast—all he can do
is try to taste a bit of everything.

WHAT'S IN A NAME?

Four years later, he sits at a different table,
weighing an offer:
"I'll pay you twenty dollars!"
  That's what his sister Freda, away at Fordham University,
    promised if he would write her term paper
      comparing two poets:
        Robert Frost and Carl Sandburg.
          Freda knows he reads poetry; she knows

Freddy writes his own poems, too.
But no one has ever *paid* him to write.
So . . . he stays up half the night, getting
    every sentence just right.
Freda pays in cash, twenty dollars.
    (*Twenty dollars!!*)
Next day, he takes all of it
downtown, buys the used typewriter
    he's seen
in the store window.
No money left for the bus,
he lugs the heavy machine uptown,
block after block after block.
Back in the basement apartment
    he shares
with some artist friends, he sets
it down, runs his fingers over the
keys, twists in a single sheet of
paper. He sits back and lets the past few
    years wash over him:
Father's death; sisters grown up,
    gone off;
the city of Pittsburgh evicting half of
    the Hill
to build some civic center;

Mother's fury at his quitting school,
    joining
the army (but then quitting that, too);
his falling in love with a Bessie Smith
    record
and the rhythm and lyrics of the blues;
his string of jobs as gardener,
    dishwasher, cook;
his constant reading of poetry books
and scribbling of verses on napkins and
    paper scraps.
This month he will be twenty, a grown
    man.
He has already left his mother's house,
already left parts of his childhood
    behind.
But what should I take from the past
through the door of this next decade?
I see myself as a writer—but does the world
see me that way?
Fingers on the keys—*tap-tap-tap. Tap-tap.*
He types out every combination of his
    name:
Frederick A. Kittel, Fred A. Kittel,
    Frederick A. Wilson, A. Wilson . . .

AUGUST WILSON.

Yes, this one. This is who I am.

POET OF THE HILL

Here he comes down Centre Ave—white shirt, tweed coat, and fancy tie.

Hey, August! Where you get those clothes?
"Thrift shop. Fifty cents."

August walks on, relaxing into his day off
from dishwashing at the diner, reciting lines
from *The Collected Poems of Dylan Thomas:*

"When I was a windy boy and a bit
and the black spit of the chapel fold . . ."

the stained-paged, dog-eared book
tucked in his pocket (the author pictured
with white shirt, tweed coat, fancy tie).
At noon, he settles onto a stool at some eatery—
Eddie's, Moose's, or the White Tower—orders
a large coffee and spends the rest of the day
filling his legal pad with verse lines and stanzas, then spilling
on to the backs of a stack of paper napkins.
People point. Whisper. Stare.

Some hot soup or a sandwich before he wanders
down to Pat's Place—the newsstand and pool hall where he
buys a cheap cigar and makes himself
invisible, listening to stories of old railroad porters:

>*Five ball in the side pocket. Hey Nate, you still got your Pullman hat?*
>*Oh, yeah, somewhere Lucille got it up in the attic. I oughta look after it, I guess.*

A halo of smoke encircling his head, August attends,
his mind like a magnet,
grasping each word that is said.

Finally, he rises, walks up Erin Street to Wylie Avenue,
meets a friend at Fish 'n' Chips.
They eat, the friend leaves, but August
hangs around outside,
leans on a street sign and eavesdrops
on the four men seated on milk crates and folding chairs
inside the jitney station—joking, talking, arguing.

>*Well, that's my business, not nobody else's.*
>*Yeah, I know, but when you come in here like that, you make it my business!*
>*Come on, now, he just young . . . he's learnin' . . .*

To a fatherless son, this man talk is a gift
from the Hill's tribal elders, warriors who survive
in this hard world.
And his job as a poet? To keep them alive.

ART ON CENTRE AVENUE

His friends have made these paintings
that say in line, color, and form
what he says in words. People are coming
in now to see them—talking, pointing, admiring.

A lone saxophone player stands in the corner,
notes filling the room like beautiful smoke.
When he takes a break, August takes
his place, picks up the rhythm with poems.

People listen. Smile. Even clap a little.
He likes this—young people, old people,
the neighborhood coming together for art.
He will do this again the next week and the next,

and then someone will offer him fifty dollars
to read his poems at a fashion show.
His confidence grows. He knows he needs
to be unique, yet speak to the whole society.

He helps to start a magazine, *Connection*—
a word that's all about how the "I" becomes "we,"
how the artist becomes the voice, the spirit
of his own community.

Every day August writes poems. He is a poet.
His friend Rob Penny writes plays in which
things happen and characters talk.
"How do you make them talk?" August asks.
"Oh, you don't—you listen to them," Rob replies.
But what does that **mean**? he wonders.
August knows nothing about plays and has seen
only one play his whole life.
Still, when Rob Penny suggests,
"Let's start a theater company!"
August replies, "Sure, why not?!"

They call it Black Horizons Theater.
August is the director. He goes to the library
and reads a book about how to direct.
Tickets are fifty cents each.
Rob and August rent a small room
and work odd jobs to pay for food.
August is proud of Black Horizons Theater,
but he still prefers poetry over drama and visual art.

He writes a story in poetry about a man named Black Bart.
"You should make that into a play," says his friend Claude Purdy,
who is a director from Minnesota.
"I can't write plays, man," August tells Claude.
But Claude is stubborn, like a dog with a bone:
"You should try. You should just do it."

A few days later . . . August decides to try. He sits
down and spreads his poems across the floor.
He picks a page in "Black Bart" where someone is saying
something interesting to someone else,
and that's where he starts.

GOIN' UP NORTH

He works on that play all day, every day for a week.
He sends it to Claude to read. He waits.

Finally, Claude calls. "I like your play. It needs some work, but I like it.
Why don't you come out here to St. Paul?"

August goes. He brings his hat, gloves, and coat.
So . . . I can write a play. Maybe I'll stay in Minnesota after all!

The Science Museum hires him to write history scripts,
little skits like "How Spiderwoman Taught the Navaho to Read."

Plays, he discovers, are like puzzles for which he has to make
the pieces. More and more, he thinks about Pittsburgh—
the streets and yards, the people and their proud, familiar voices.

VOICES

He leans over the blank page, listening.
Who's there?
A man—no, a few men. One older.
Two veterans. A car. A phone on the wall.
Bringggg! Brinnnggg! Brinnnngggggggg!!!
    It's the jitney station on Wylie Avenue,
next to the Fish 'n' Chips where he liked to hang out,
    eavesdropping on the men.
"Yeah, we take you up there—no taxis will go there, but we sure do!'"
    The young men strut and argue, the old ones reminisce.
Way up in Minnesota, August listens, scribbles down some lines:
    Who are they? What are they saying . . . and why?

BITS AND PIECES

"Look at this," Claude says, slapping the book
down on the table in front of August.
So—he looks. And looks and looks and *looks.*
He's seen art: sketches on sidewalks, framed
paintings his friends made in Pittsburgh, he's even seen
famous paintings from Europe in library books.
But not like this—not like the art of Romare Bearden
(a name that suggests a king with copious chin hair)—
with its bits and pieces of newspapers, magazines, foils,
and fabrics, cut paper, painted paper, and oh, my lord . . .
look at those smokestacks, rural shacks, trains, and windows—
look at those roosters, snakes, birds, and cats!
And over here, see those big hands, that conjure woman?
And here . . . those drums and that guitar?

August spends all night with that book, savoring
the bits and pieces in Bearden's art
showing him how a whole world can flower
from some small, single thing.

A VERY GOOD RECIPE

He quits his job at the Science Museum, but he doesn't quit
writing. At the soup kitchen Little Brothers of the Poor,
he peels potatoes, boils peas, mops the floor.
He watches the men and listens, passing out buttered bread,
but the voices in his head
are from Pittsburgh, jitney drivers whose own lives
have come to less than they expected:

"I'm just tired . . . Can't hardly explain it . . . you look up one day
    and all you got is what you ain't spent."

At night, he piles up pieces of scrap paper and napkins
scribbled with dialogue and scenes,
a collage of human voices.
He reads them, crosses out, rearranges.
Now he has a cast of black characters, spread across his floor,
asking August to be sure
they will be seen—and heard.

PROCESS

"How do you make them talk?" August once asked
his friend Rob Penny about the characters in his plays.
"Oh, you don't—you listen to them," Rob had replied.
Now, August understands what that *means*.
He listens to those voices from the Wylie Avenue
taxi station. He writes them into scene after scene.
Finally, he has a play he calls *Jitney* that he sends
to a national playwright's conference.
He gets a reply.

"Thank you for submitting your play to us, Mr. Wilson.
We did not choose your play . . ."
"Rejection is part of the artist's process," Claude tells him.
"Try again."

OK, August thinks, peeling potatoes at
Little Brothers of the Poor. He writes some more.
He sends *Jitney* to the Playwrights' Center in Minneapolis.
And what do they send back . . . ?

"We accept your submission, Mr. Wilson.
Here is your check for twenty-five hundred dollars."

ARRIVING

I.
Pittsburgh, 1982. He wears a
white shirt, tweed coat, fancy tie.
Daisy wears her best dress.
Mother and son get into the jitney—
a freelance taxi that drives in the Hill
because no downtown taxis will—and ride over
to where actors of the Allegheny Repertory Theater
are performing *Jitney*—a play by August Wilson.

2.

Back in Minnesota, August hears a new
group of voices: a blues singer and her musicians.
He writes down what they say and what they do,
arranging and rearranging scenes
like Romare Bearden making a collage.
Ma Rainey, his next play, is finished.

3.

October 1984: *Ma Rainey* opens on Broadway
in New York City. August watches people
crowding into the theater, filling the rows
of seats, whispering excitedly.
Lights dim, darken. The play begins . . .

CYCLE

He walks two blocks from the restaurant
where he's been writing on notepads
and sipping coffee.
Inside, he brushes the Minnesota slush from his shoes,
removes his hat and gloves, shakes out the cold.
These hands are almost forty years old, he thinks.
Four times ten years. Four decades—
an easy way to slice up your life (though life isn't so easy to slice!).
But in art, everything's a tool, and August has a goal:
Write one play for each decade of the twentieth century,
a map of the black experience in America.
He's already working on the next one
about a hardworking father, a former
Negro League Baseball Player, his wife and son.
August spreads the handwritten pages across the table.
He is back in the Hill District of Pittsburgh, listening . . .
Who's there?
What are they saying . . . and why?

> "I CRAWL UP INSIDE THE MATERIAL, AND I GET SO IMMERSED IN IT
> THAT AS I'M INVENTING THIS WORLD, I'M ALSO BECOMING A PART OF IT."
> —AUGUST WILSON

AUTHOR'S NOTE

I write about creators who use their personal landscape and daily experience as inspiration. Poet-physician William Carlos Williams wrote about sparrows, plums, wheelbarrows, and house calls. WWI veteran Horace Pippin painted trenches and grenades—but also living rooms, backyards, and kitchens. Composer Olivier Messiaen used local birdsong in his famous *Quartet for the End of Time*, which he penned in the bathrooms of a German prison camp. Painter Georgia O'Keeffe scavenged bones in the New Mexico desert, transforming them into astonishing art.

August Wilson, too, mined the raw materials of his own life to fuel his creative fire. The ten plays in his *Pittsburgh Cycle* are based on his childhood and early adult memories of the Hill District with its vibrant mix of people, places, and street-savvy vernacular. When I first saw *Seven Guitars* and *Fences* performed at my local theater, I was completely captivated by the mythic qualities of the characters and their poetic dialogue, inspired by Wilson's habit of listening closely to the voices of people in his own neighborhood. Both plays were intense, raw, passionate—and tragic. Afterwards, as I read about Wilson's childhood and his self-education at the Carnegie Library of Pittsburgh (which, in October 1989, gave him a diploma to acknowledge it), I knew I had to share his story with young people.

My research for this book included visiting the Hill District of Pittsburgh and the Carnegie Library, watching both live-staged and recorded versions of Wilson's plays and interviews, speaking with actors, and reading countless news articles, books, and reviews. It became apparent, as I immersed myself in these materials, that the full arc of his creative life might be too much for a picture book. I decided, therefore, to focus primarily on his early years: his journey from curious, observant child to angry teen dropout to self-taught poet to Broadway playwright and two-time Pulitzer Prize winner. By placing black culture squarely in the center of the stage, his impact on American theater and the African American community remains profound and reverberates through today's generation.

Wilson based two of his plays, *Joe Turner's Come and Gone* and *The Piano Lesson*, on paintings by the collage artist Romare Bearden and credits Bearden with providing the example for his own organic process. As I worked on Wilson's story, I kept the playwright's quote above my desk: "I just write stuff down and pile it up, and when I get enough stuff, I spread it out and look at it and figure out how to use it." As a nonsequential thinker and as a writer who often spreads her manuscripts down the hallway or across the living room floor—I was cheered by the playwright's faith in intuition and his insistence on "listening" to his characters. I tried to listen, too. I used Wilson's own words where I could, and where I could not, I wrote spoken lines based on what I thought he and others would say in that situation.

I hope the readers of this book will appreciate the richness of their own lives and neighborhoods and have the courage to listen to the voices they find there—and perhaps like Freddy/August be inspired to write about them.

—Jen Bryant

TIME LINE

April 27, 1945 Frederick "Freddy" August Kittel is born in Pittsburgh, Pennsylvania. He is the first son and fourth child of six born to Daisy Wilson, an African American cleaning woman, and Frederick Kittel, a white German baker who is absent for much of the children's lives. Daisy, an intelligent and resourceful woman, raises her family in a small apartment on Bedford Avenue in the then-thriving, multicultural Hill District, known as Little Harlem.

1949 Having been forced to leave school after sixth grade, Daisy emphasizes literacy with her children. By age four Freddy is reading independently.

1950 Daisy takes Freddy to the Hill District Branch of the Carnegie Library where he obtains his first library card. *Curious George* is his first borrowed book.

1951–52 Freddy attends Pittsburgh Public School in the Hill District and then Holy Trinity School.

1953–57 Attends St. Richard's Roman Catholic School (later St. Benedict the Moor School) on Bedford Avenue until the first part of seventh grade. Sixth grade teacher Sister Christopher encourages his writing.

1957 Daisy divorces Kittel and moves the family to a rented house in the steelworkers' neighborhood of Hazelwood. She marries David Bedford, who will later partly inspire the character Troy Maxson in *Fences*. Freddy attends St. Stephen's parochial school through eighth grade.

1958–59 While idolizing black boxers like Charley Burley and Sonny Liston, Freddy also discovers black writers such as Paul Dunbar, Langston Hughes, and Richard Wright at the Hazelwood Branch of the Carnegie Library. He begins to read the thirty or forty books in the "Negro section," many of which will influence his thinking and his writing.

1959–60 Freddy attends the all-white Central Catholic High School where he's bullied because of his color. He fights back but eventually transfers to Connelly Trade School, where he's bored by the weak academics. He then transfers to Gladstone Public High School, where he's accused of plagiarizing a paper he wrote on Napoleon. He drops out in frustration and, afraid to disappoint Daisy, spends school hours at the main branch of the Carnegie Library.

1962–63 Enlists in the U.S. Army for three years but leaves after the first.

1964 Works a variety of odd jobs including cook, dishwasher, and gardener.

1965 Biological father, Frederick Kittel, dies. Freddy writes a term paper for his sister and earns twenty dollars, which he uses to buy a typewriter. He changes his name to August Wilson, moves into a boarding house in the Hill District, and begins to write poetry. He begins to listen to blues recordings, which he will later claim are "the wellspring of [his] art."

1966–67 Lives among artists, works in restaurants, and continues to read and write poetry. At local diners and cafés, he writes verses in notebooks and on napkins. At a cigar store, Pat's Place, he listens to old railroad porters tell their stories. Cofounds *Signal* magazine (later renamed *Connection*).

1968 Rob Penny convinces August to be the director for their new community theater, Black Horizons, whose aim is to raise black consciousness in Pittsburgh. Having no theater experience, August reads about directing in a library book. Black Horizons Theater stages several plays by Rob Penny, Amiri Baraka, and Ed Bullins.

1969 Stepfather, David Bedford, dies. August marries Brenda Burton; they will divorce in 1972.

1970 Daughter Sakina Ansari Wilson is born.

1973–76 Sees his first professional play, *Sizwe Bansi Is Dead* by Athol Fugard. Still focused on poetry, Wilson also writes short stories and a few one-act plays (*Recycle*, *The Homecoming*, and *The Coldest Day of the Year*) for amateur community theaters. At the urging of his friend Claude Purdy, he writes *Black Bart and the Sacred Hills*, a play based on his poems.

1977 Visits Purdy in St. Paul, Minnesota, and decides to stay. Gets a job writing for the Science Museum of Minnesota. Discovers Romare Bearden, whose paintings and artistic method become a major influence.

1977–79 Quits Science Museum job and works as a cook for Little Brothers of the Poor.

1979 Remains in St. Paul but increasingly draws on his Pittsburgh roots for inspiration. Writes *Jitney*, a play based on a freelance taxi service in the Hill District. Submits *Jitney* and *Black Bart and the Sacred Hills* to the O'Neill National Playwrights Conference but is rejected.

1980 Writes another Pittsburgh-inspired play, *Fullerton Street*, submits it to the O'Neill but is rejected. Submits *Jitney* to the Minneapolis Playwrights' Center and receives a fellowship.

1981 Marries Judy Oliver, a social worker.

1982 *Jitney* performed at the Allegheny Repertory Theater in Pittsburgh. O'Neill National Playwrights Conference accepts *Ma Rainey's Black Bottom*, Wilson's play about a legendary blues singer. Director Lloyd Richards and Wilson begin a working partnership that will last for decades.

1983 Daisy Wilson dies. Wilson's play *Fences* given staged reading at O'Neill National Playwrights Conference.

1984 *Ma Rainey* performed at Yale Repertory Theater, directed by Lloyd Richards. Wilson's play *Joe Turner's Come and Gone* (inspired by the Romare Bearden painting *Mill Hand's Lunch Bucket*) read at the O'Neill Center's National Conference. In October *Ma Rainey* opens on Broadway in New York City at the Cort Theatre and runs for 285 shows.

1985 *Fences* premieres at Yale Repertory Theater. *Ma Rainey* wins the New York Drama Critics' Circle Award. *Jitney* performed at Penumbra Theatre, St. Paul, Minnesota.

1986 *Joe Turner's Come and Gone* opens at the Yale Repertory Theater. The play's setting is a Pittsburgh boardinghouse.

1987 *Fences* (whose main character, Troy Maxson, is a Pittsburgh sanitation worker and former Negro League Baseball player) opens on Broadway. It wins Wilson his first Pulitzer Prize, Tony Award, and his second New York Drama Critics' Circle Award.

1988 *Joe Turner's Come and Gone* opens on Broadway and *The Piano Lesson* (Wilson's second play inspired by a Bearden painting) opens in Boston. *Joe Turner* wins the New York Drama Critics' Circle Award (Wilson's third).

1989 *The Piano Lesson* premieres at Yale Repertory Theater. *Pittsburgh Magazine* names Wilson the 1990 Pittsburgher of the Year.

1990 *The Piano Lesson* opens on Broadway. *Two Trains Running* (set in 1969 Pittsburgh, a diner in the Hill District), which wrestles with issues of racial inequality, civil rights, poverty, and urban renewal, opens at Yale Repertory Theater. Wilson wins his fourth New York Drama Critics' Circle Award and his second Pulitzer Prize for *The Piano Lesson*. Divorces Judy Oliver and moves to Seattle, Washington.

1991–92 *Two Trains Running* is produced in Seattle, San Diego, Washington, DC, Los Angeles, and New York (Broadway.) It wins the New York Drama Critics' Circle Award.

1994 Marries Constanza Romero, a costume designer. *The Piano Lesson* is filmed as a teleplay in Pittsburgh and airs on the Hallmark Hall of Fame.

1995 *Seven Guitars* (set in the backyard of a boardinghouse in Pittsburgh in the 1940s), the last of Wilson's plays directed by Lloyd Richards, opens in Chicago. Wilson is inducted into the American Academy of Arts and Letters.

1996 After being produced in Boston, San Francisco, and Los Angeles, *Seven Guitars* opens in New York and wins the New York Drama Critics' Circle Award. Wilson receives the William Inge Distinguished Achievement in the American Theater Award (Independence, Kansas). He gives a landmark speech, The Ground on Which I Stand, at a biennial theater conference at Princeton University.

1997–99 Daughter Azula Carmen Wilson is born. Wilson debates Boston critic Robert Brustein regarding multiculturalism in the theater. A revised version of *Jitney* opens in New Jersey. Wilson receives the National Humanities Medal. *King Hedley II* premieres in Pittsburgh.

2000–02 *King Hedley II* opens in Los Angeles; Boston; Washington, DC; Chicago; and New York. *Jitney* appears off-Broadway and wins the New York Drama Critics' Circle Award. Wilson is writer in residence at O'Neill National Playwrights Conference.

2003–04 Actress Whoopi Goldberg appears in *Ma Rainey*; Phylicia Rashad appears in *Gem of the Ocean*—both on Broadway. Wilson given Chicago Tribune Literary Award for lifetime achievement.

2005 Yale Repertory Theater premieres Wilson's final play in his ten-play cycle *Radio Golf*. He is diagnosed in June with terminal cancer and dies in a Seattle hospital on October 2. At funeral services in Soldiers & Sailors Memorial Hall, Pittsburgh, actor Charles S. Dutton reads a line spoken by Troy Maxson, the main character of *Fences* "Death ain't nothin' but a fastball on the outside corner. That's all death is to me." Wilson is buried near his mother in Greenwood Cemetery, Pittsburgh.

NOTES

Title note: "Feed Your Mind, the Rest Will Follow: An Op-Ed Column" appeared in the *Pittsburgh Post-Gazette*, March 28, 1999. It is the text of Wilson's address of March 18, 1999, at the 100th anniversary of the Hill District branch of the Carnegie Library.

ACT ONE
The Hill District, Pittsburgh
"If you can read, you can do anything . . .": B.S. Flowers, ed., *Bill Moyers: A World of Ideas*. New York: Doubleday, 1989 (p. 170).

"When It Rains, It Pours"
"Morton Salt!" and "Tell them I said no . . .": Dinah Livingston, "Cool August: Mr. Wilson's Red-Hot Blues." *Minnesota Monthly*, vol. 21, October 1987 (p. 28).

Relocation
"Nigger Stay Out": Ibid. (p. 26).

Detour
"Be proud, my Race, in mind and soul . . .": Excerpt from "Ode to Ethiopia" by Paul Laurence Dunbar, *The Complete Poems of Paul Laurence Dunbar*. New York: Dodd, Mead and Company, October 1913 (p. 15).

Schooled
"Go Home Nigger": John Lahr, "Been Here and Gone." *New Yorker*, April 16, 2001 (p. 56).

Prove It!
"I'm going to give you one of these two grades . . .": John

O'Mahony, "American Centurian." *Guardian*, December 13, 2002 (see theguardian.com/stage/2002/dec/14/theatre.artsfeatures).

ACT TWO

Rows
"I dropped out of school, but I didn't drop out of life": August Wilson, "Feed Your Mind, the Rest Will Follow." *Pittsburgh Post-Gazette*, March 28, 1999 (see old.post-gazette/magazine/feedmind.asp).

"I always tried to go in everyone's way . . . what I called myself": Ralph Ellison, *Invisible Man*. New York: Random House, Modern Library edition, 1952 (p. 433).

Poet of the Hill
"Thrift shop. Fifty Cents": Lahr, "Been Here and Gone" (p. 58).

"When I was a windy boy and a bit/And the black spit of the chapel fold . . .": Excerpt from "Lament" by Dylan Thomas, *The Collected Poems of Dylan Thomas*. New York: New Directions, 1957 (p. 194).

"Well, that's my business . . . he's learnin'": Author's words loosely based on lines in act one, scene three, of *Jitney* (1982).

Friends Can Be Persistent
"How do you make them talk?" and "Oh, you don't—you listen to them": Ben Brantley, "Theater: The World That Created August Wilson." *New York Times*, February 5, 1995, sec. 2, pp. 1–5 (see nyti.ms/2fCwDFQ).

"You should make that into a play": David Savran, *In Their Own Words: Contemporary Playwrights*. New York: Theatre Communications Group, 1988 (p. 291).

"I can't write plays, man": Dennis Watlington, "Hurdling *Fences*." *Vanity Fair*, April 1989 (p. 108).

Goin' Up North
"Why don't you come out . . .": Ibid.

Voices
"Jitneys" or "gypsy cabs" were unlicensed taxis that delivered passengers to and from areas of the city where licensed taxi drivers refused to go.

Bits and Pieces
Two of Wilson's plays, *The Piano Lesson* and *Joe Turner's Come and Gone*, began with a single image from Romare Bearden's paintings. However, those particular images were not in this first book of Bearden's that Wilson saw.

A Very Good Recipe
Little Brothers of the Poor is a social services organization founded in Paris after World War II. The Minneapolis/St. Paul chapter opened in 1971. Wilson worked there as a cook.

"I'm just tired . . . what you ain't spent": Lines spoken by the character Becker in *Jitney*, act one, scene two (1982).

Arriving
Sections 1, 2: This is 1982; August Wilson is thirty-seven years old. Section 3: *Ma Rainey* opened at the Cort Theater on Broadway in October 1984.

Cycle
"Write one play for each decade of the twentieth century": Wilson achieved this goal. The last of his ten-play "cycle," *Radio Golf*, premiered at the Yale Repertory Theater in April 2005. Wilson died on October 2, 2005.

"He's already working on the next one . . .": Refers to *Fences* (1985).

Author's Note
"I crawl up inside the material . . .": Bill D. Moyers, *A World of Ideas* (Betty Sue Flowers, ed.). New York: Doubleday, 1989 (p. 178).

Opposite Page
"I left Pittsburgh . . .": From "Feed Your Mind, the Rest Will Follow: An Op-Ed Column." *Pittsburgh Post-Gazette*, March 28, 1999 (see old.post-gazette.com/magazine/feedmind.asp).

Copyright Page
"I don't write for black people or white people . . .": Vera Sheppard, "August Wilson: An Interview," from *Conversations with August Wilson* (Jackson R. Bryer, Mary C. Hartig, eds.). Jackson, MS: University Press of Mississippi, 2006 (p. 109).

SELECTED BIBLIOGRAPHY

Books
Bigsby, Christopher, ed. *The Cambridge Companion to August Wilson*. Cambridge, UK: Cambridge University Press, 2007.

Bryer, Jackson R., and Mary C. Hartig, eds. *Conversations with August Wilson*. Jackson, MS: University Press of Mississippi, 2006.

Glasco, Laurence A. and Christopher Rawson. *August Wilson: Pittsburgh Places in His Life and Plays*. Pittsburgh: Pittsburgh History & Landmarks Foundation, 2015.

Herrington, Joan. *I Ain't Sorry for Nothin' I Done: August Wilson's Process of Playwriting*. New York: Limelight Editions, 1998.

Kolin, Philip C., ed. *American Playwrights Since 1945: A Guide to Scholarship, Criticism, and Performance.* New York: Greenwood Press, 1989.

Nadel, Alan, ed. *May All Your Fences Have Gates: Essays on the Drama of August Wilson.* Iowa City: University of Iowa Press, 1994.

Washington, M. Bunch, intro. by John A. Williams. *The Art of Romare Bearden: The Prevalence of Ritual.* New York: Harry N. Abrams, Inc., 1974.

Articles

Churnin, Nancy. "The Academic and the Dropout," *Los Angeles Times*, February 6, 1988.

DeVries, Hilary. "A Song in Search of Itself," *American Theatre*, January 1987, vol. 3, no. 10, 22–5.

Dorman, John L. "August Wilson's Pittsburgh," *New York Times*, August 15, 2017.

Dyer, Ervin, and Monica Haynes, "Real-Life Drama Surrounds Wilson's Childhood Home," *Pittsburgh Post-Gazette*, January 26, 2003.

Freeman, S. G. "A Voice from the Streets," *New York Times Magazine*, May 15, 1987, 36–50.

Lahr, John. "Been Here and Gone," *New Yorker*, April 16, 2001, 50–65.

Malehorn, David. "How I Found August Wilson's Carnegie 'Diploma,'" *Pittsburgh Post-Gazette*, October 9, 2011.

Wilson, August. "Feed Your Mind, the Rest Will Follow: An Op-Ed Column," *Pittsburgh Post-Gazette*, March 28, 1999.

Film/Video

August Wilson interview with Charlie Rose, shortly after the opening of *Seven Guitars*, March 25, 1996. See youtube.com/watch?v=7vb9Vg_WGi0.

"August Wilson: The Ground on Which I Stand," PBS, February 24, 2015. See pbs.org/video/2365429059.

"The Piano Lesson," directed by Lloyd Richards, Hallmark Hall of Fame, (TV premiere) February 5, 1995. Hallmark Home Entertainment (DVD) December 17, 2002.

"A World of Ideas: Writers" Interview with Bill Moyers, Season 1, Ep. 14, Athena Studios, 1991. Available on Amazon at amzn.to/2uNzCkJ or on Vimeo at vimeo.com/33300464.

Websites

National Endowment for the Humanities
neh.gov/about/awards/national-humanities-medals/august-wilson
    Article about Wilson for his 1999 NEH Medal Award.

PBS's American Masters
pbs.org/wnet/americanmasters/august-wilson-the-ground-on-which-i-stand-scenes-and-synposes-of-august-wilsons-10-play-cycle/3701
    Play highlights, interview clips, Wilson biography, and time line.

Pittsburgh Music History
sites.google.com/site/pittsburghmusichistory/pittsburgh-music-story/jazz/hill-district
    Archival photographs, maps, and a brief history of the heyday of the Hill District and its rapid decline after the urban "renewal" of the 1960s.

Pittsburgh Post-Gazette
old.post-gazette.com/pg/03001/497623.stm#table
    Archive of Wilson's hometown newspaper, the Pittsburgh Post-Gazette, with links to interviews, articles, photos, and more.

Historic Hill Institute
historichill.org
    Preservation Organization of the Hill District neighborhood of Pittsburgh, Pennsylvania, with information about events and tours.

PLAYS BY AUGUST WILSON
(Dates written in parentheses)

Recycle (1973)
Eskimo Song Duel: The Case of the Borrowed Wife; An Evening with Margaret Mead; How Coyote Got His Special Power and Used It to Help the People. (date unknown; unpublished; written for the Science Museum of Minnesota)
Black Bart and the Sacred Hills (1977)
Fullerton Street (written 1980; not produced)
The Homecoming (1989)
The Coldest Day of the Year (1989)
How I Learned What I Learned (2002)

AUGUST WILSON'S PITTSBURGH CYCLE
Ten plays, each one set in a decade of the twentieth century (Dates first performed in parentheses)

Gem of the Ocean—1900s (2003)
Joe Turner's Come and Gone—1910s (1986)
Ma Rainey's Black Bottom—1920s (1984)
The Piano Lesson—1930s (1987)
Seven Guitars—1940s (1995)
Fences—1950s (1985)
Two Trains Running—1960s (1990)
Jitney—1970s (1982)
King Hedley II—1980s (1999)
Radio Golf—1990s (2005)

"I LEFT PITTSBURGH, BUT PITTSBURGH NEVER LEFT ME."
—AUGUST WILSON

"I don't write for black people or white people; I write about the black experience in America. And contained within that experience, because it is a human experience, are all the universalities."

—AUGUST WILSON

To all the young people, searching the rows: May you find your mentors there!
—J. B.

To my mom, for all her love and support
—C. C.

Thanks to Jennifer Pickle Styran, Carnegie Library of Pittsburgh; Marylu Denny, director of membership services, and Karen Cahall, docent, Pittsburgh History and Landmarks Foundation; Liz Simpson, assistant registrar, Detre Library and Archives, Heinz History Center, Pittsburgh; Leigh and Kurt Skvarla, generous hosts, Wexford, Pennsylvania; Melanye Finister, actor, People's Light theater company, Malvern, Pennsylvania; Deborah Taylor, coordinator of school and student services, Enoch Pratt Free Library, Baltimore; the research staff at the Smithsonian Library, Washington, DC; Jenn O'Leary, Dana McDonnell, and Kacey Doran at the FHG Library, West Chester University, West Chester, Pennsylvania; and Carol Welch and Laura Salvucci, reference department, Chester County Library, Exton, Pennsylvania.

And for their incredible patience and wisdom, my thanks to Tamar Brazis and Howard Reeves, editors, and Amy Vreeland, managing editor, at Abrams Books for Young Readers, and to my wonderful agent Alyssa Eisner Henkin, VP at Trident Media, LLC. And finally, to Cannaday Chapman, whose extraordinary art I first spied in the *New York Times*—what an honor and a pleasure to work with you!　　—J.B.

The author pledges a portion of the royalties earned from the publication of this book to the Daisy Wilson Artist Community, for the purpose of restoring August Wilson's childhood home in the Hill District and providing a creative community space. Visit Daisywilson.org.

The art in this book was created using a variety of materials: ink, colored pencil, acrylic paint, and cut paper. The final layouts were assembled and colored in Adobe Photoshop.

Cataloging-in-Publication Data has been applied for and may be obtained from the Library of Congress.

ISBN 978-1-4197-3653-7

Text copyright © 2019 Jen Bryant

Illustrations copyright © 2019 Cannaday Chapman

Book design by Chad W. Beckerman

Printed and bound in China

10 9 8 7 6 5 4 3 2 1

Abrams Books for Young Readers are available at special discounts when purchased in quantity for premiums and promotions as well as fundraising or educational use. Special editions can also be created to specification. For details, contact specialsales@abramsbooks.com or the address below.

Abrams® is a registered trademark of Harry N. Abrams, Inc.

ABRAMS The Art of Books
195 Broadway, New York, NY 10007
abramsbooks.com